A·LITTLE
New
England
Cookbook

Barbara Bloch

ILLUSTRATED BY
SUSAN DAVID

First published in 1991 by
The Appletree Press Ltd, 7 James Street South,
Belfast BT2 8DL.
© 1991 The Appletree Press Ltd.
Illustrations © 1991 Susan David used under
Exclusive License to The Appletree Press Ltd.
Printed in China. All rights reserved.

First published in the United States in 1991
by Chronicle Books, 275 Fifth Street,
San Francisco, CA 94103.

ISBN: 0-87701-879-0

9 8 7 6 5 4 3 2

Introduction

Much of the present day cooking of New England can be traced to the English origin of the settlers who landed on Plymouth Rock and to the kind of food they found in the area when they arrived. As the Pilgrims struggled for survival during the first hard winters, they were helped by Native Americans who knew the land so well. The settlers were taught how to grow and cook the food of the region and to hunt and fish Indian-style. They learned that sugar (often in the form of maple syrup) provided added protection for the body during the bitter cold winters, which is why many traditional English dishes have come down to us sweeter than the original versions. Native corn, pumpkin (considered peasant food at that time in Europe), other squash, cranberries, beans, maple syrup, turkey, and cod were among the foods found by the Pilgrims when they arrived in "New" England.

A note on measures
Spoon and dry measurements are level. Seasonings can of course be adjusted to taste. Recipes are for four unless otherwise indicated.

Blueberry Muffins

My husband and I spend our summer vacations on an island off the coast of Massachusetts. When we first went there, we stayed at a place called Blueberry Hill Farm, named for the lush blueberries growing on the property. Blueberries grow in profusion throughout New England and, when they are in season, we eat them fresh and use them to make all kinds of wonderful treats.

---

2 cups all-purpose flour	1 egg, beaten
1/2 cup sugar	1 cup buttermilk
2 1/2 tsp baking powder	1/3 cup vegetable oil
1/2 tsp each baking soda	1 1/2 cups fresh blueberries
and salt	2 tbsp all-purpose flour
butter to serve	
(makes 12 muffins)	

Preheat oven to 400°F. Grease 12-cup muffin pan. Place dry ingredients in large bowl and stir to combine. Place egg, buttermilk, and oil in separate bowl and beat until well blended. Make well in center of dry ingredients and pour in egg mixture. Stir just until dry ingredients are moistened (batter will be lumpy). Toss berries in 2 tbsp flour and fold into batter. Spoon batter into muffin cups, filling them 2/3 full. Bake 20 to 25 minutes. Remove from pan immediately and serve hot with butter.

Blueberry Pancakes with Maple Syrup

New England is as famous for its maple syrup as for its plump, delicious blueberries. Real maple syrup is special. It costs more than imitation syrup, but the flavor is so much better, it's worth the cost. When served with pancakes or waffles, maple syrup should be heated gently and served hot. Once opened, the syrup must be refrigerated, but, if it is refrigerated too long, it will turn to sugar. A maple syrup producer solved this problem for me by suggesting I keep extra syrup in the freezer where it will keep almost indefinitely.

1 3/4 cups all-purpose flour	2 eggs, beaten
2 tsp baking powder	4 tbsp melted butter
1/2 tsp salt	1 cup fresh blueberries
1 1/4 cups milk	hot maple syrup and butter to serve

(makes about ten 4-inch pancakes)

Sift dry ingredients into bowl. Stir in milk, eggs, and butter. Beat until smooth. Fold in blueberries and pour into pitcher. Lightly grease griddle and heat until drop of water dances on surface. For each pancake, pour about 4 tbsp batter onto griddle and cook until bubbles appear on surface. Turn with spatula and cook until browned on second side. Serve immediately with hot syrup and butter.

Cranberry Quick Bread

The climate of Cape Cod provides ideal growing conditions for cranberries. They were so precious to early settlers that a law was passed in 1773 prohibiting the harvesting of cranberries before September 20th. Cranberries and blueberries are interchangeable in most recipes. The only difference is that cranberries are more tart than blueberries and usually require additional sugar.

---

2 cups all-purpose flour	1 1/2 cups cranberries, coarsely chopped
1/2 cup granulated sugar	1 cup chopped walnuts
1/2 cup firmly packed light brown sugar	1 egg, beaten
1 1/2 tsp baking powder	1 cup orange juice
1 tsp each baking soda and salt	3 tbsp vegetable oil

(makes 1 loaf)

Preheat oven to 350°F. Grease 9- x 5-inch loaf pan. Sift dry ingredients into bowl. Stir in cranberries and nuts. Combine remaining ingredients and stir into dry ingredients just until moistened. Pour into pan and bake 1 hour or until cake tester inserted into center of bread comes out clean. Cool in pan on wire rack 10 minutes. Remove from pan and cool completely on rack.

Boston Brown Bread

This bread traditionally is made in 1-lb coffee cans. But these days coffee often comes in 13-oz cans. Since it is evidently the amount of coffee that has changed more than the size of the can, you can use whichever size you have. Serve bread with Boston Baked Beans (see page 24).

---

1 cup cornmeal
1 cup stirred whole-wheat flour
1 cup sifted rye flour
2 tsp baking soda
1 tsp salt
2 cups buttermilk
6 tbsp molasses
1 cup seedless raisins
butter or cream cheese to serve

Place dry ingredients in bowl and stir. Combine buttermilk and molasses, make well in center of dry ingredients, and add mixture. Stir just until dry ingredients are moistened. Add raisins. Grease 2 coffee cans (see above). Spoon batter into cans, filling them $2/3$ full. Grease 2 pieces of aluminum foil and place, greased side down, securely over cans. Place cans on rack in large saucepan. Pour in enough boiling water to come halfway up sides of cans. Cover pan and simmer $1^1/2$ to 2 hours or until cake tester inserted in bread comes out clean. Add additional water as necessary to maintain water level in pan. Cool cans on wire rack 2 minutes. Remove bread from cans and cool completely on rack. Slice when cool and serve with butter or cream cheese.

Lobster Rolls

Summertime along the coast of New England is vacation heaven for anyone who loves the ocean, the dunes, and the beach. Living is informal and much of the eating is casual. Few vacationers want to change out of beach clothes at lunchtime, and they don't have to. Open-air lunch stands are easy to find near the beach, and Lobster Rolls are always on the menu. You can make your own Lobster Rolls at any time of the year. Or, if you prefer, you can substitute shrimp or crabmeat for the lobster.

---

2 cups diced, cooked lobster meat
$1/3$ cup diced celery
$1/2$ small onion, diced
about 4 tbsp mayonnaise
4 drops hot pepper sauce
salt to taste
4 frankfurter rolls
mayonnaise for spreading
potato chips and bread-and-butter pickles to serve

Place lobster meat, celery, and onion in a medium-size bowl. Add mayonnaise and toss gently. Season with hot pepper sauce and salt. Spread rolls with mayonnaise and fill with lobster salad. Serve with potato chips and pickles.

Clams on the Half Shell
or Steamed Clams

New Englanders are particularly fond of clams. Softshell clams are often served as "steamers" for a very casual meal or first course. Hardshell clams, or quahogs — also known as littlenecks or cherrystones — are delicious served raw. Be sure to remember, however, in these days of unending water pollution, that it's vital to purchase clams from a very reliable fish market.

To serve quahogs on the half shell, they must be very fresh, well scrubbed, and very cold. Be careful not to lose any of their delicious juice during shucking. Place open clams, about 6 per person, on a bed of cracked ice and serve with wedges of lemon, horseradish, freshly ground pepper, or cocktail sauce if you must.

To serve steamers, buy about 2 dozen softshell clams per person. Scrub thoroughly under cold running water and place in large saucepan. Add $1/2$ inch salted or sea water (don't use unsalted water). Cover tightly and cook just until clams open, about 8 minutes. Discard any clams that don't open. Remove with slotted spoon and place in large bowl. Strain broth and pour into cups. Melt butter and pour into small dishes. Fingers are the only efficient way to proceed. Diners help themselves to clams from the large bowl, open them, dip them in clam broth and then into melted butter. When clams have been eaten, the delicious broth is drunk carefully so sand that has washed off the clams remains in the bottom of the cup.

Fish Chowder

New England clam chowder is justly famous. An equally delicious chowder, however, can be made with less expensive fish that's available all year. Substitute a dozen clams for fish if desired and, if you want a thinner soup, eliminate the flour or add additional milk or cream.

---

2 lbs cod or haddock fillets
2 tbsp butter
1 onion, chopped
2 tbsp all-purpose flour
2 cups milk
2 medium-size potatoes, cooked, peeled, and cubed
1 cup heavy cream
4 slices bacon, cooked, drained, and crumbled
salt and freshly ground pepper to taste
paprika and freshly chopped parsley to garnish
oyster crackers to serve
(serves 6)

Cook fish in 2 cups water 15 minutes until fish flakes easily. Remove with slotted spoon and break into small pieces. Strain and reserve liquid. Melt butter in large saucepan, add onion, and cook until transparent. Stir in flour and cook 3 minutes. Add fish liquid and milk slowly, stirring constantly. Cook until slightly thickened. Stir in fish and potatoes. Simmer until heated through. Add cream, bacon, and seasoning. Heat gently. Garnish with paprika and parsley. Serve with oyster crackers.

Pumpkin Soup

When the early settlers made pumpkin soup, they had no choice but to use fresh pumpkin that had to be peeled, diced, cooked, and puréed. You can still make it that way, but it's a lot easier to start with canned pumpkin purée. Although purists may not agree, I think it tastes just as good. Pumpkin Soup can be served either hot or cold. To serve cold, chill thoroughly, and stir well before serving.

---

2 tbsp butter
1 small onion, finely chopped
2 cups pumpkin purée
2 1/2 cups chicken stock
2 1/2 cups light cream
1 tsp lemon juice
1/2 tsp each sugar and salt
1/8 tsp ground cloves
hot pepper sauce to taste
4 tbsp dairy sour cream and freshly chopped parsley to garnish

---

Melt butter in large saucepan. Add onion and cook until transparent. Stir in pumpkin and simmer 5 minutes. Add chicken stock, stir well, and cook over low heat about 15 minutes. Add remaining ingredients except sour cream and parsley, stir, and cook just until heated through. Spoon into bowls, and top each serving with 1 tbsp sour cream. Sprinkle with parsley and serve immediately.

Cheddar Cheese Soup

Vermont is justly famous for its delicious Cheddar cheese. Originally it was referred to as "rat" cheese, a term viewed with nostalgic affection by those who find much of the processed cheese sold in supermarkets an unfortunate excuse for "real" cheese. The cheese can be served appropriately for any course and can be eaten at any time of day.

---

3 tbsp butter
¹/₂ small onion, finely chopped
1 small carrot, finely chopped
¹/₂ small green pepper, finely chopped
1 small celery stalk, finely chopped
1 clove garlic, minced
3 tbsp all-purpose flour
4 cups chicken stock
³/₄ lb sharp Cheddar cheese, shredded
3 cups milk
salt and hot pepper sauce to taste
croutons and freshly chopped parsley to serve
(serves 8)

Melt butter in large saucepan. Add vegetables and cook until softened. Stir in flour and cook 3 minutes. Add stock slowly, stirring constantly. Add cheese and cook, stirring, until melted. Stir in milk and season to taste. Simmer gently until heated through. Garnish with croutons and chopped parsley.

New England Clambake

An old-fashioned New England Clambake, invented by native American Indians, is like no other picnic in the world. The new settlers were quick to recognize the advantages of cooking by this method and copy it. Almost the only thing that has changed over the years is the many foods that have been added to the original menu, which, as the name implies, was primarily clams.

Per person you will need:
about 1 dozen scrubbed clams
1 lobster
$1/4$ to $1/2$ broiler/fryer chicken
1 or 2 ears freshly picked corn
1 or 2 scrubbed potatoes
about 4 small white onions, peeled
additional food, if desired, such as: sausage; flat fish; turnips,
peeled and cut into chunks; sweet potatoes
(melted butter, hot rolls, salad, beer, soda, watermelon to serve)

Clambakes are usually held on a beach where a large pit can be dug for cooking. Early in the day the "bakemaster," and anyone willing to help, digs a deep pit big enough to hold all the food. The pit is lined with large, flat, dry rocks and a roaring fire is built over them. The fire must burn two or three hours until the rocks are red hot. While the fire is burning, cooks get to work preparing the food. Husks are peeled back, from the corn, silk is removed, and husks are pulled back over the corn. The different kinds of food are placed in separate cheesecloth bags. When the fire has burned down to ash the embers are raked. A thick layer of wet seaweed is placed over the rocks and the bags of food are placed on top of the seaweed immediately so no precious steam is lost.

The food is covered with another thick layer of wet seaweed and the seaweed is covered with a large tarpaulin. Rocks are placed at the corners of the tarpaulin, and sand is used to cover the edges so steam can't escape. Now the wait begins. It will be one or two hours before the food is ready — the perfect time for a swim. In about an hour and a half, a corner of the tarpaulin is turned back and the food tested for doneness. When everything is finally cooked, the tarpaulin is lifted and the feast begins — starting with clams dipped in melted butter, and ending with wedges of cold watermelon. Chances are you'll eat more than you ever thought possible. But when the food is gone, you can relax on the beach, listen to waves rolling in from the ocean, and look forward to another clambake.

Homemade Boston Baked Beans

Many colonists were deeply religious and would not permit work on the Sabbath. As a result, dishes like baked beans were popular because they could be cooked ahead of time and served hot or cold. Bake them uncovered long enough to get a good crust on top and, by all means, serve them hot.

---

1 pkg (16 oz) dried navy beans or Great Northern beans	1 tbsp dry mustard
1 onion, chopped	2 tsp allspice
4 to 6 tbsp ketchup	salt and freshly ground pepper to taste
3 to 4 tbsp each brown sugar and molasses	1/4 lb salt pork, rinsed and slashed

(serves 6)

Place beans and 6 cups lightly salted water in saucepan. Bring to a boil and cook 3 minutes. Cover and let stand 1 hour. Preheat oven to 300°F. Drain beans and place in 2 1/2=quart casserole. Combine remaining ingredients except pork and stir into beans. Pour in boiling water to cover beans, bury pork in beans, cover and bake 5 1/2 hours, stirring occasionally. Add additional water during cooking as necessary to keep beans moist. Bake uncovered during last 1/2 hour. Discard pork if desired. For variety, add sliced frankfurters to leftover beans before reheating.

New England Boiled Dinner

This classic recipe has changed very little over the years. Most recipes instruct the cook to boil beets in a separate saucepan, which makes sense. Opinions are about evenly divided, however, on the question of whether the remaining vegetables should be cooked with the meat or cooked separately. Both methods work, but I prefer to cook vegetables with the meat because it makes them more flavorful.

---

1 corned beef brisket, about 5 lb
8 medium-size potatoes, peeled
8 carrots, scraped and cut in half
1 medium-size turnip, peeled, cut in half, and sliced
16 small white onions, peeled
1 large head cabbage, cored and quartered
8 medium-size beets, cooked, peeled, and sliced
horseradish sauce, mustard pickles, and mustard to serve
(serves 6 to 8)

Place corned beef in large, deep pot and cover with cold water. Bring to a boil and skim surface to remove scum. Reduce heat, cover, and cook until meat is fork-tender, about 3 hours, adding additional water during cooking as necessary. About 30 minutes before meat is done, add potatoes, carrots, turnip, and onions. About 15 minutes later add cabbage. Reheat beets if necessary. When everything is tender, drain, slice meat, place on platter, surround with vegetables, and serve with horseradish sauce, pickles, and mustard.

Oyster Stuffing

Although early Thanksgiving feasts undoubtedly included wild turkeys, it's unlikely they were stuffed with oysters. But oysters were plentiful in Colonial times, and it may be that early settlers eventually used them to stuff fowl. Oyster stuffing is certainly popular today and often is used to stuff a modern Thanksgiving turkey.

---

7 cups oysters in liquid	1 egg, beaten
1 cup butter	4 tbsp freshly chopped parsley
1 medium-size onion, chopped	2 tbsp ground sage
1 1/2 cups chopped celery	salt and freshly ground pepper
25 slices stale white bread,	to taste
crusts removed and cubed	

(enough to stuff a 12–16 lb turkey)

Drain and coarsely chop oysters, reserving liquid. Place oysters in large bowl. Melt butter in saucepan, add onion and celery, and cook until softened. Add to oysters with remaining ingredients

and mix well. Add enough reserved oyster liquid to make a slightly moist mixture. Spoon into prepared turkey cavity just before cooking, or spoon into baking dish, cover, and bake about 45 minutes in oven preheated to 325°F.

Boiled Lobster

From the time colonists arrived in New England until close to the turn of this century, lobsters were so abundant that they were used as bait. But times have changed and today lobsters are an expensive treat. When cooked and eaten at home, however, they usually cost less than a dinner of less exciting fare at a restaurant. Lobster can also be served cold with lemon wedges and mayonnaise. Lobster cooking in our family is my husband's responsibility. Lobsters must be purchased alive and, from that point until they are placed on the table ready to eat, I am only too happy to turn the cooking, simple as it is, over to my husband.

One 2 lb lobster per person is a good weight. Fill large pot with enough water to cover lobsters. Add 1 tbsp salt for every quart of water. Bring water to a rolling boil, and drop lobsters into water head first. Cover and wait for water to return to a boil. Simmer 15 to 18 minutes. Plunge lobsters into cold water to stop cooking. Twist off claws. Split down underside of tail, crack claws, and serve with lemon wedges, lots of melted butter, and a good supply of paper napkins.

Vineyard Bay Scallops

The first time I visited Martha's Vineyard off the coast of Massachusetts — more years ago than I care to remember — the friend I was visiting, our daughters, and I spent a wonderful morning collecting scallops from the lagoon in front of our house. Then, while the children napped, we spent hours opening the shells to remove the scallops. After spending so much time, you would have thought we would have more scallops than we could possibly eat. Wrong! Although we'd had lots of fun, we still had to buy some for dinner. My husband and I stay at a house on the same lagoon, but these days we buy our scallops at a local market.

---

1 lb bay scallops
4 tbsp butter
1 1/2 cups dry bread crumbs
2 tbsp each snipped chives and freshly chopped parsley
2 tsp fresh lemon juice
salt and freshly ground pepper to taste

Preheat oven to 375°F. Place scallops in single layer in small buttered baking dish and set aside. Melt butter in a small skillet, add remaining ingredients, and stir until well combined. Spoon over scallops and bake about 20 minutes or until top is nicely browned.

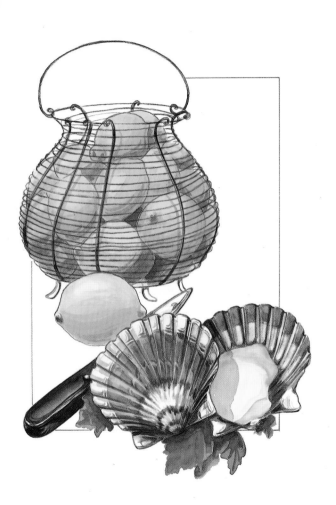

Tarragon-Chicken-Oyster Pie

Colonists protected egg-producing chickens because eggs were so highly valued. By the time one of their chickens ended up in a pie, it was likely to be old and rather tough. Fortunately young, tender chickens are easily available today, as, much of the time, are oysters.

---

3 whole chicken breasts, boned, skinned, poached and cubed
24 shucked oysters
lemon juice
2 tsp tarragon
salt and freshly ground pepper to taste
2 tbsp butter
2 tbsp all-purpose flour
2 cups milk
pastry for 1-crust pie
milk for brushing pie crust
(serves 6 to 8)

Preheat oven to 400°F. Butter 2-quart round casserole. Arrange chicken and oysters in casserole. Sprinkle with lemon juice and seasonings. Melt butter in saucepan. Stir in flour and cook 3 minutes. Add milk slowly, stirring constantly. Cook over low heat until thickened. Season to taste. Pour sauce over chicken and oysters. Cover casserole with pastry and crimp edges. Brush lightly with milk. Bake 30 minutes.

Codfish Balls

There's a finger of land off the coast of New England called Cape Cod for the plentiful cod that is found in that coastal region. The discovery that cod could be salted, and thereby preserved for long periods, made it an economic cornerstone in the l7th century. A carving of the "Sacred Cod" was hung in the Massachusetts Hall of Representatives in l784, and it's still there! You can use fresh or salt cod in the recipe that follows. If you use salt cod, soak it in cold water overnight.

---

l lb fresh cod fillets
about 5 medium-size potatoes, cooked and mashed
l egg, beaten
4 tbsp butter
l tbsp Dijon-style mustard
l tsp Worcestershire sauce
salt and freshly ground pepper to taste
l small onion, finely chopped
2 tbsp freshly chopped parsley
vegetable oil to cook and tartar sauce to serve

Poach cod in lightly salted water until it flakes easily. Drain, cool, and flake. Combine with potatoes and remaining ingredients except oil. Shape into l$\frac{1}{2}$-inch balls. Heat oil in deep-fat fryer to 375°F. Fry balls until golden, about 3 minutes. Remove with slotted spoon and drain on paper towels. Serve with tartar sauce.

Hashed Brown Potatoes

Maine produces more all-purpose potatoes than any other state. If possible, sauté the potatoes in a non-stick pan.

---

about 4 tbsp butter, more as needed
4 medium-size potatoes, firmly cooked, peeled, and diced
I onion, chopped
salt, freshly ground pepper, and paprika to taste
freshly chopped parsley to garnish

Melt butter in skillet. Add potatoes and onion. Season and cook until browned on bottom. Turn with spatula, add additional butter as necessary, season, and cook until browned on second side. Garnish with parsley.

Acorn Squash New England-Style

This winter squash can be stored safely for long periods, a boon to settlers who had few ways to preserve food.

---

2 acorn squash
4 tbsp maple syrup
2 tbsp each butter and dry sherry
nutmeg, salt, and freshly ground pepper to taste

Preheat oven to 375°F. Cut squash in half and scoop out seeds. Place, cut side up, in baking dish. Divide remaining ingredients equally in squash halves. Pour I cup water into dish and bake 50 minutes or until fork tender. Baste with syrup several times during cooking. Drain off water and serve.

Corn on the Cob

Corn can be divided into three categories: corn grown as animal feed — not intended for human consumption; corn boxed and shipped to a supermarket — not, in my opinion, fit for human consumption (although plenty of people eat it); and deliciously edible corn bought at a local farm stand within a few hours of picking. As soon as corn is picked, the sugar in it starts to turn to starch and its sweet natural flavor begins to diminish. So, by the time corn reaches a supermarket, it tastes no better than (and sometimes not even as good as) corn that comes from a can. Years ago my father grew corn in his vegetable garden. We would put a pot of water on to boil shortly before dinner and then go into the garden to pick corn. I remember that freshly picked corn as the best I have ever eaten.

In mid-July, farm stands, scattered around the countryside in New England, start to sell local corn. When it's in season, buy at least 2 ears of corn per person. Remove the husks and silky threads. Bring a large pot of lightly salted water to a rolling boil, and add about 1 cup milk and 1 or 2 tbsp sugar. Place corn in boiling water and cover. (Watch pot to be sure water doesn't boil over.) Once water returns to a boil, cook 5 minutes — no longer. Remove corn with tongs, place on platter, and wrap in large napkin to keep warm. Serve with lots of butter, salt, and freshly ground pepper. Very fresh corn cooked this way is truly wondrous eating.

Harvard or Yale Beets

The traditional rivalry between Harvard and Yale extends even to the way beets should be cooked! The Harvard version is made with vinegar; the Yale version is made with a mixture of orange and lemon juice. I had no idea there was more than one version of this recipe, and for years I made "Yale" beets and called them "Harvard" beets. Now that I know, I won't make that mistake again, or I'm likely to get into trouble with Yale and Harvard graduates in the family.

$^1/_2$ cup cider vinegar
or
$^1/_2$ cup orange juice plus I tbsp lemon juice
$^1/_2$ cup sugar
2 tsp cornstarch
12 small beets, cooked, peeled, and diced
2 tbsp butter
salt and freshly ground pepper to taste

(serves 6 to 8)

Place vinegar (for Harvard) or orange and lemon juice (for Yale) in medium-size saucepan. Stir in sugar and cornstarch. Bring to a boil and simmer 5 minutes. Add prepared beets and cook until heated through. Stir in butter and season to taste.

Quick Succotash

Corn and beans were among the many vegetables grown in America before the Pilgrims arrived. They adapted the word "succotash" from the Indian word "m'sickquatash," meaning hulled corn, and they copied the Indian custom of cooking several different kinds of food together in one pot. There are many ways to make Succotash. You can use dried, fresh, or frozen beans — limas or others; you can add tomatoes or use cream; you can add onion; you can add salt pork or bacon. But if you want to make Succotash, you must always start with corn and beans.

---

4 tbsp butter
I small onion, chopped
I pkg (10 oz) frozen baby lima beans, cooked
I pkg (10 oz) frozen corn kernels, cooked
$^1/_2$ cup heavy cream
salt and freshly ground pepper to taste
freshly chopped parsley to garnish
(serves 6)

Melt butter in medium-size saucepan. Add onion and cook until onion is transparent. Stir in lima beans and corn. Add cream and season with salt and pepper. Stir to combine and cook over low heat until heated through. Garnish with chopped parsley.

Beach Plum Jelly

If you have never been to Cape Cod, the islands of Nantucket and Martha's Vineyard, or along the Northeast coast, you may never have heard of beach plums. They grow on bushes near the ocean and are a small, sour fruit used only to make jelly. Jars of this much prized jelly are sold in New England, but I have rarely seen them sold elsewhere.

Collect ripe, firm beach plums. Wash and remove stems and place in large, heavy saucepan or kettle. Barely cover with water. Cover saucepan and simmer until plums are tender. Pour into cheesecloth or jelly bag set above large bowl. Don't mash or squeeze fruit, it will make the jelly cloudy. Allow liquid to drip several hours or overnight until all liquid has come through bag. Measure liquid and return to a clean saucepan. Add I cup sugar for every I cup juice. Bring to a boil slowly, stirring until sugar has dissolved. Reduce heat and simmer, uncovered, until jelly reaches 220°F. Pour into properly sterilized jars and set aside at room temperature until jelly has begun to set. Cover with melted paraffin. When paraffin has solidified, add second layer of paraffin or lid of screw-top jar. Once a jar has been opened, store in refrigerator.

Note: Never make jelly on a rainy day. It won't set properly.

Cranberry Conserve

It's hard to think of cranberries without thinking of Thanksgiving. Cranberries and turkey go together much the way bread and butter go together. Fresh berries are only available in the fall, but they freeze beautifully, so I buy extra and keep them in the freezer to use all year. I make this conserve every Thanksgiving and just about any other time I cook turkey.

---

4 cups cranberries
2 oranges, unpeeled
1 cup seedless raisins
2 cups sugar
1 cup chopped nuts (almonds, walnuts, or pecans)
4 tbsp brandy
(makes about 1 quart)

Place berries in large saucepan, add water, and cook, uncovered, until berries begin to pop. Skim surface to remove scum. Cut oranges and remove stem ends and seeds (don't peel). Place in food processor with raisins and process just until coarsely ground. Add to cranberries and stir. Add sugar and stir until sugar is dissolved. Cook, uncovered, about 15 minutes or until thickened. Remove from heat and stir in nuts and brandy. Cool to room temperature and store in refrigerator. If conserve is not intended for immediate use, pack in hot, properly sterilized jars and seal. Once jar has been opened, store in refrigerator.

Strawberry-Rhubarb Pie

The taste for rhubarb is very American. It's almost invariably served as a dessert although it is, in fact, a vegetable. The leaves are poisonous, so be careful not to eat them. The stalks, however, have a remarkable and unusual tart flavor that some people have a passion for and others don't like at all. Rhubarb is a popular addition to many home gardens. It's available fresh in late spring and summer and available frozen all year.

---

pastry for 2-crust 9-inch pie	3 tbsp all-purpose flour
3 cups rhubarb pieces, about ¹/₂ in long	¹/₄ tsp each nutmeg and salt
	2 tbsp butter
I cup sliced strawberries	milk for brushing
1¹/₂ cups sugar	
(serves 6 to 8)	

Preheat oven to 375°F. Line bottom of 9-inch pie plate with half of the pastry. Place fruit, sugar, flour, and seasonings in bowl and toss gently. Spoon into pastry-lined pie plate and dot with butter. Cover with remaining pastry and brush with milk. Bake 45 to 50 minutes. Place on wire rack to cool. Serve warm or well chilled.

Pumpkin Pie

Thanksgiving, that thoroughly American holiday, was begun by Pilgrims who felt there should be a special day to give thanks. Whether Pumpkin Pie was on the menu that first Thanksgiving is debatable, but pumpkin surely was served in one form or another. There is, however, no doubt that Pumpkin Pie is traditional at modern Thanksgiving feasts.

---

pastry for 1-crust 10-inch pie
2 cups pumpkin purée
3/4 cup firmly packed light brown sugar
1 tsp cinnamon
1/2 tsp each ground ginger and nutmeg
1/4 tsp each ground cloves and salt
3 eggs, beaten
1 1/2 cups light cream
whipped cream flavored with chopped
crystallized ginger to serve
(serves 8 to 10)

Preheat oven to 425°F. Line 10-inch pie plate with pastry. Place pumpkin purée in large bowl. Stir in seasonings. Add eggs and cream and stir well. Pour into pastry shell and place carefully in center of oven. Bake 15 minutes. Lower oven to 350°F and bake 30 minutes or until sharp knife inserted into center of pie comes out clean. Place on wire rack to cool. Serve warm or chilled with dollops of whipped cream.

Indian Pudding

This dessert, probably the most famous in New England, is made with cornmeal. It would be logical to assume it got its name because Indians taught the colonists how to make it. Not so! The name comes from the fact that early settlers called corn "Indian corn" to distinguish it from wheat, which they, and their British brethren, called corn. All of which is almost as confusing as the number of different recipes there are for Indian Pudding.

5 cups milk	1/2 tsp each ground ginger,
5 tbsp yellow cornmeal	ground cinnamon, and salt
I cup molasses	2 eggs, beaten
4 tbsp butter	flavored whipped cream or
	ice cream to serve

(serves 8)

Preheat oven to 350°F. Grease 1 1/2-quart round baking dish. Place 4 cups of milk in top of double boiler and bring to a boil directly over heat. Add cornmeal slowly, stirring constantly. Place pan over simmering water and cook 15 minutes, stirring frequently. Add molasses, butter, and spices. Stir until well combined. Remove from heat. Add small amount of hot mixture to beaten eggs, stirring constantly. Pour warmed egg mixture back into pan slowly, beating constantly. Spoon into baking dish and pour remaining milk on top. Don't stir! Bake 1 hour. Serve hot with whipped cream or ice cream.

Blueberry Grunt

Few things are more colorful, or confusing, than the many names Americans have invented to describe fruit desserts. There is, of course, the familiar term "pie". There are also Slumps, Grunts, Pandowdys, Bettys, Buckles, Cobblers, Crisps, and probably some I never heard of. The name used depends on which New England state you come from or which cookbook you read. What one cook calls a Cobbler, another calls a Buckle or Slump. A Slump and a Grunt are really the same thing — a cooked fruit dessert topped with dumplings or biscuits.

---

3 cups blueberries	3 tbsp maple syrup
4 tbsp sugar	3 tbsp lemon juice
1/4 tsp each ground cinnamon and nutmeg	

Biscuit Topping:

1 cup all-purpose flour	4 tbsp butter, softened
2 tbsp sugar	1 egg, beaten
1 1/2 tsp baking powder	about 5 tbsp milk
1/4 tsp salt	

flavored whipped cream to serve
(serves 6)

Preheat oven to 375°F. Place berries in 1 1/2-quart baking dish. Combine sugar and spices, sprinkle over berries, and toss gently. Drip maple syrup over top and sprinkle with lemon juice. Bake 5 minutes. Remove from oven and raise heat to 425°F. To make topping, sift dry ingredients together and blend in butter. Stir in egg and add as much milk as necessary to make soft dough. Drop dough by tablespoonfuls over berries. Bake 25 minutes or until crust is well browned. Serve hot with whipped cream.

Drinks

Here are two drinks — one, cool and refreshing, to enjoy after a day at the beach, the second to share with friends around a blazing fire on a cold New England evening.

Cranberry Juice Cocktail

l quart cranberry juice	4 tbsp honey
2 cups orange juice	2 cinnamon sticks

(serves 6)

Combine all ingredients in large saucepan, bring to a boil, reduce heat, and simmer about 5 minutes. Remove cinnamon sticks, pour into large pitcher, and place in refrigerator until thoroughly chilled. Serve over ice.

Hot Mulled Cider

3 cinnamon sticks	$3/4$ cup firmly packed
10 whole cloves	brown sugar
2 quart apple cider	$1/2$ tsp each nutmeg and
	ground ginger

(serves 12)

Enclose cinnamon sticks and cloves in small cheesecloth bag. Place in large saucepan with remaining ingredients. Bring to a boil, reduce heat, and simmer about 10 minutes. Discard cheesecloth bag. Ladle into cups and serve hot.

Index